Pressing Olives

Prayers & Poems

CRADLE PRESS

Pressing Olives
Prayers & Poems

ISBN: 978-0-9789499-8-3

Library of Congress Control Number: 2015943512

This book is printed on acid free paper.

*For my parents
and my sister, Pam*

Contents

12 Hours of Daylight

absent by night
the joys of day did grow
Your light lacking, Lord
slumbers my restive soul

my will yet lumbering
hoists the world up brittle vines
in my untended garden
of unintended time

fail me not when I fail
to praise Your Name as Word
to listen as You lead
in hours of faith disturbed

and when again I stumble
then try once more my climb
make me holy, humble
unto Your will divine

let dreams of You
alight my nights
hold me close
in days of light

Prophet Named

I am the porous rock
I am the still water
dire in dreams
cloistering calamity
my name is Wisdom
my name is Prophet
I am many in one
and one in many
upon whom the Lord bestows
the sacred invitation

I proffer holy momentum
heaving the centuries
to the foot of the Cross
where harbingers of destruction
failed to slay seers of Truth
no fires devour salvation
no lions' den divides
nor hellish horrors deceive
dragons burst into spates of pitch and fat
dry bones rattle and reassemble
shrines are silenced
by secret screams shattering idols

scorned by kings dethroned
the one King rises
His hailing messengers marveling
one Truth
by His lofting love was I named
to serve Him was I saved
to speak His mercy
on lips pressing together

every letter of every alphabet
every word of every tongue
every time of every place
a faith lineage unbroken
the remnant restored

my God is loyal
and by my life
loyalty I return
I live and die downstream
His revelation prophesy
returns the promise
upstream towards Eden
awakening the mystery of the first regeneration
knowledge retrieved then carved
onto parchment portioned
into confetti of Divine punctuation
love language
Logos evangelization

Rend to Render

Lord, rend gently my hardened heart
wash my wounds in Your refulgence
love my doubts away
rest me assured of reunification
mend my lacerations
repair me through hope
of saintly purification
render me Your fervent witness

Me First Then You

I rock my sins to sleep
while You sing lullabies of forgiveness

I weep for my weeping
while You wane the tears

I nail my limbs to a beam of steel
while Your Cross bends it in the wind

I ravage goodness for my own possession
while You lead my heart to serve

I shun temperance to act in haste
while You convey tender reminders

I punish myself by harming others
while You mend me with grace

I lose my place in the must trust plan
while You shepherd me to surrender

I neglect to praise and worship
while You honor my heart with humility

I confuse the mysterious for chaos
while You lend me witness to glory

I put me first then You far in the future
while You even before creating me
put me first then You

Curse to Bless

let to tremble the blood red moon
weep to spare the stars
gloom and anguish drip
from dying darkened skies
fields aflame
locusts trample
all Zion in despair

scattered is your heritage
portents' terrible day
repent that He will relent
return to the mountains of mercy

trumpet the fast
of great and glorious day
gather assemble
bless and rouse
survive to be called

judgment drowns
in early rain's abundance
the sweet milk slips
over blades of swords and spears

plowshares share
the warrior covenant
the day of every generation
of the Lord's children

will prophesy
see dreams
dream visions

there is no other God
He will pour out His Spirit blessing

Towards the Fire

Lord,
endow me with enduring charity
make me the child
that makes Your peace
place me in the world
reach through me to others
remind me always
to search my prayers
and there discover my heart
sustaining compassion
ever opening towards the fire
of Your inextinguishable mercy

Winter Prayer

woods in wind
sticks stuck to snow
streams descending
deciphering winter

devotion befalls me
I have no breath
but Yours, Lord

kindle my fire of ice
hissing honeycombed lava
thaw me to hollow
melt me to move
ardently into Your will
Word and way

make still my prayer
fever me in fog
wane the morning
of my wasted hours

guide my daylight
grace my place
hold me whole
in Your holy skies

carve me in accordance
shape me to Your Name

Advent

in the weary waiting
the severity of His absence
one last gasp of penitence
no life within to spare
in prayer we prepare

each soul a fitting repository
rife with anticipation
longing for arrival
liberation denied
until one silent star
heralds celestial coronation

our need for a Savior gestating
the water of catholicon breaks
majesty awash
coming to us
the child is born to bear
death's prerequisite grace

Emmanuel leading
we follow expectant

Just Beyond Violet

the word Jerusalem
lives in our lexicon like a cave
a safe place where we return
again and again
in the visible spectrum
to a larger and unified event
our foundation
the heart of a world of completeness
healed and sound
guiding pillar of vision
protection of the righteous
reign of peace of Lamb of God of salvation
exalted above the hills
the Lord shall see

Spring

all green and supple
is the spring
which lo before my heart
God brings
and in His love I sing
I sing

Mary

Crucifixion reconciled
by yearly beauty springtime
Mother of radiance
all flowers bloom on your behalf
filling up our windows
paned framed hazel
magnolia pink dignity
glory gray sky
O Clement Apparition
blessed art Thou
most gracious Assumption
ripened by reverence
adorned ignited
sunlighted
haloed not thorned
with stars not scars
mother to every flowering reed
fragrant heavenly confidence
moss green maternal love
lily of the sacred valley
returning happiness
all petals opened to the Son

Palm Sunday, Mexico

weaved palms from the marketplace
Christ dying on the cross
Christ living in a halo

holding the eclipse in his mouth
the ancient serpent priest
tests the rain the sun the moon
marks his days

Amen

folds his hours

Amen

measures his years
from inside a blackened cave

Amen

skeletal palm shadow
waving into the future
a Man
a marker of every solstice
a dweller in every cave
Hosanna braided
into the hands of humankind

Fishers of Men

the sun casts rays
without expectation
fishermen cast lines
baiting fervent hope
fishers of men reel in
Apostolic promise

Poverty of Spirit

upon You
for all I rely
even my dependence on You
is dependent on Your love

my words form prayers
flowing within
Your Word
initiating my prayer

no action of mine
can I will to act
if Your will
will not allow action

my impatience
is bound to Your timing
restless until You lead me
into timeless You

all suffering I can endure
only if You weaken me
emptied by You
my conversion made strong

Your Passion
redeems my suffering
joined with Yours
lifted to You lifting me

by Your gift
I am graced with gratitude
and so can bless and offer
all I am to Your I AM

tempered and taught
guided and guarded
Your plan in me
my plan surrendered

the light I breathe shines in threads
spools of connective oxygen
pulling and releasing
me to You
You to me

Angelic Almanac

the days were preaching heat
the nights in starry acclamation
time confined years
gave way to rosary decades
the beads of hours praying through us
our gentle Mother's mantel
shelters as we toil and till
while crop dusting angels
shimmer dewy iridescence
upon the living fields
blessing the soil
where we plant and sow
under flights of flocks in favor

Species

in the garden
by the cup
mystical agony
translated
into species

Pressing Olives

You whispered me
towards the garden
hand picked me
Your olive to press
I did not oblige
clinging instead
to convincing inconveniences
encouraging isolation

my moment's pause
faced the craggy hill
the chalky hush of Gethsemane
gazed in tender wishing

from opposite the Mount
I leaned on stones
fortress walls willingly accepted
an incalculable distance between us
I refused to traverse

You other and same
pressing me without pressure
malaxing me into You
defying the gravity of separation

little did I know
that in my garden of desperation
Your grace is the singular prayer
the indispensable step
to awaken droplets of my love
to combine

even in remembrance
I am helpless to help
to comfort You in the agony

You did not pass the cup of abandonment
from which You anoint me to love You
the chalice of reverent sacrifice
You willed to the Father

if I can press from olives
all hand picked moments
redemptive and willing
build in me
the bravery of walls that crumble

Wandering

Praise and thanks, O Gracious God
as we wander along
Your constant trail
of unexpected grace

directing us daily
Your generosity
the gift of our conversion

weighted shame we carry
every hounding sin
loosening rocks beneath our feet

release us
into releasing
the rolling hills of our regrets
reconciled by benevolent rainfall
quenching the thirst in our hearts

encouraged towards courage
we lose our voices
and are emptied to echo
the entirety of our resounding
YES

Nicodemus

darkness and light
Nicodemus by night
water wind
spirit flight

Pentecost

promised Spirit
infusion of the New Covenant
peace be with you
breathe on us
the power of forgiveness
the prophecy already granted

we cannot wish away
our inevitable creation
our certain death

the Paraclete
renovates the recurring dream
of souls in sin perishing
to peace and comfort indwelling

fifty days after
the playing fields of birth and death
are rekindled
made level by fire

Sighs Too Deep

Come, Holy Spirit
remove this film of tears gone dry
envision us in Your perfection
make us not bashful to obey
beckon saintly intercession
heal these self inflicted wounds
but leave us scars
remembrance of selfish visibility

clear the path of clarity
that we may proceed
in righteousness rather
than in sins gathered
quell our defiance
hurry us humble
reveal to us the gift
that makes the giver
take from us our taking

alight in us prayerful calm
rest us in purity by Your Word
let us not fail to praise
or falter to magnify
Your radiant revelation
plain in sight
and invisible

Salved

Loving God
Triune and triumphant
take my desire's
long longing for You
keeper of my soul
keep me Yours
salved in stillness
poised for sanctification

Holy Shroud

flicker of travertine
blackness of tomb
silence buries sound
darkness traps light
space cradles form

faint and mysterious
whispers on threads
resting atop fibrils
a reflection of suffering imbued
the totality of human sin
particles of pain
held together
by particles of peace

the scandal of doubt subsists
questions asked
theories posed
controversy masked
an image on a cloth reposed

carbon locks
readable time
unlocking
reachable faith
the gift paramount
millions venerate
science investigates

perhaps in the ethereal hovering
an event horizon
His body floating

everlasting and marvelous waves
lighting His every sacrifice
connecting the dots
framing the grid
mapping our sins
into slats of spheres
cylindrical specters that vector

perhaps the residue of His rising lingers
like a subatomic chameleon
imprinting cloud-like layers
transparency indicators
of helix horizontals
webbed verticals
quanta order
the chaos illusion
now you see it
now you don't

perhaps instead
photons chatter and agree
their polarization angles identical
instantaneous spatial orientation
crisscrossing ripples
into subtle order
where all particles commit
to nonlocality
and matter is sanctified
in living radiation

in the sacred tomb
the heartbeat of death
does not negate creation
nor does the heartbeat of creation
negate death

we collapse by design
into the Divine
interconnectedness
and the unbroken flowing
prayer in panorama

human frailty trembles
in dimensions undefined
particle subtlety ascension
density unwinds

His gift of peace serene
on cloth suspended
our dream

Lead Me to Discern

that You will my ongoing conversion
and that what You will not
is not mine to decide

reverberate in me
unlimited devotion
direct my words
to worship and praise

enunciate my prayers
that I may always call You forth
articulate my love for You my loving King

grace me by way of Truth
guide me subside me

teach me by entirety
in action and reflection
in contemplation and prayer

steer me to obey
walk and choose Your way

restore me
to Your design
preserve me
by Divine Providence

ready me within Your loving creation
into a sacred conversation

bend my knees
before the Cross of invitation
Your mercy triumphant

Incorruptible

Syria in shards
Damascus hemorrhaging refugees
rubble reminiscent
of Paul at Lystra
stoned and left for dead
dragged through dust and rocks
still breathing
the blinding light that sees

Calvary quakes
earthen cracks crumble
rocks rub sparks
to singe the weeds of sin
seeds of forgiveness take hold
blooming absolution
budding ransomed love
so that upon this rock
Apostolic restitution imbibes
the blood of the Lamb
Lord Jesus

Christ the incorruptible
exposes the corruption
of the false ruler of the world
who infiltrates human imagination
tempting with illusions of control
insidious idolatry and trickery

but God cannot be deceived
thus the pernicious plan
already decomposing in pellucid darkness
will be crushed and buried
suffocated by imperishable Love

Onto All That Is Ordinary

present through presence
where we readily abide
if You so will it
by the power of Your Holy Spirit
domicile of wisdom

our eyes lean long
towards Your loving gaze
teeming the holy mystery
onto all that is ordinary
lodged in unexpected moments and places
alive in the paradoxical

curing the disposition of mind
with the balm of tranquility
bringing us into infinite intimacy
to be Your willing creation

You make our lives a wandering Gospel
in the flux of Your proximity
rooted in Your unreachable distance
we pray for the understanding
to feel our faith in You
in joyful unison with You

when we reach too far
want too much
pray too little
take all the credit
ignore those in need
hoard generosity
resuscitate us in Your Sacred Heart

where all beats of our hearts are rescued

You never abandon or shun
when our sins surface to consume
when lies chase and masquerade

every time we disregard Your will
You return our hearts
to the heart of the matter before us
You, Christ Jesus and Your Holy Church

Pointing Past Forward

the Israelites
seeking independence from Egypt
saved when following Moses
baptized in the Red Sea

the new Israel
seeking liberation from slavery to sin
saved by following Jesus
baptized in water

a young man following seized
wears nothing but a linen cloth
runs away naked
unable to be captured
the cloth left behind

a young Man followed condemned
buried in nothing but linen cloth
rises anew
able to transcend death
the burial cloths left behind

the Messianic Secret secured
the mystery revealed
more than a miracle worker
like us He suffers He dies
water mixed with blood
flows from the pierced side
of the crucified Christ

the Father accomplishes
in the fullness of time

the life and death of Jesus
the fruition of Christ's mission
during the end times

unifying the Divine plan
pointing past forward
to shared exaltation
the new Exodus to salvation

Unrepeatable Name

Your love for me

connecting all my disconnects
disconnecting all my connects
like breathing and drowning at the same time

in the lull of uncertainty
when I cease speaking
You call me
by my unrepeatable name
the entirety
You created me to be

I imagine You telling me
My child
you need never under
or over achieve

air is endless
still birds must flap their wings
loft alone is not enough
to induce flight

clouds release the rain
with no intention of quenching thirst
or growing food to nourish

Not Rather

human will to Yours
not a gesture of courtesy
rather fidelity of love

humility
not a devaluation
rather an inflation of heart

surrender
not capitulation
rather infrastructure

trust
not fearful reliance upon
rather total dependence upon

gratitude
not self-directed appreciation
rather fluency to receive

generosity
not vainglorious giving
rather the conduit for praising

God's presence
not an incursion
rather a welcome emptying

emptying
not an obedient deprivation
rather a fully willed sacrifice

fiat
not a yes demanded
rather a yes granted

who one is
not called to be oneself
rather already is and need only arrive

Clay of Gravity

the cry low deep
an edge too steep

you dive into density
the black hole
compressing mass
swallowing darkness

there the awakening
you are your own prisoner
solo
at the bottom of self
in the place of never happy

true surrender animates freedom
once you admit that alone you cannot

giving up
giving in
you plead

Lord

pull me
past panic
corner me
in discomfort
ruin me
in fear

purify me
in Your image
magnetize me
with Your might

mold my clay of gravity
transfigure me by Your light

Eucharistic Adoration

uncomfortable in the creaking pew
my mind is slow to quiet
the furnace kicks on and off
like heartbeats conversing with silence
lulling me into Your sacred rhythm

while into Your everything
everything in Your house
shifts into translucence
edged in gold
even the air is gilded
Your presence
wafting the breeze of Heaven
inflates unseen dimensions
resplendent corridors appear
emanating timeless love
the refuge of holy intimacy

for lack of oxygen
my heart panics
stops then syncs
with the perpetual vibrancy
wonder rapid in unison with awe
by reciprocity of palpitation
Your benevolent restitution
bleeds redemption
replacing hemoglobin with sacrifice

salvaged by splendor
You place me in the upper room
of Eucharistic initiation
to adore by receiving
and receive by adoring

there by the lantern
of love's forever flame
words cease
I lose track of time
bow my head
fold my hands
kneel and unwind

cherishing me
You invigorate the darkness
of my sleepwalking life
enlightening in me lasting urgency
the desire to be worthy
to serve and celebrate
You ever and all

Prayerful Warrior

sovereign Lord
make me Your warrior
meld this enduring ache into arms
these splinters
into swords drawn forth
in surrender

love me into the battle
of self trench warfare
lure my artificial strength
suffocate my resolve
so that all enemy passions
meet their violent demise

sanctify my fight
that the slippery veneer
of bloodstained foes
once untainted
are sacrificed and sainted

polish me to praise
that in Your glory
I my tarnish rid

on Your fields of friendly fire
gun me down running
convert my next desire

Like the Father

in the ether of stillness
atmospheric and silent
the gift inside grows into itself
embryonic and systemic
the umbilical heart
beats past punishment
by cadence of consolation
corporeal and spiritual

we are loved in joy
the proclamation
elated and teeming

God's mercy breathes for us
in holy transfusion
sacred sweat to blood
oxygenating our veins
with the love that pardons
born through Christ

forgiven and given
we are called
to sacrificial pilgrimage
the Church opens Holy Doors
to restoration and elevated living
Her steeples reaching for the apex
cornerstone and capstone
shore up love to love
buttressing faith
when by conversion we cross
the threshold in the asking
for mercy like the Father

readied in the Son
His blueprint of intangible interior
reified in us

the clear and cloudy
substance of our nature
inside the nature of our Creator
is the self given and received
His love living in us
is ours to live in Him
when we become the gift
requisite in His mercy
microscopic in grandiosity
in the mysterious regeneration

Ode to Trinity

while the day away comes near
I hold my night in present fear
and reach to God a tender trill
no cloud no bird
no sound no shrill

for in tall grasses once I lay
stars above me waking day
and in the sun His holy ray
breaking bread and wine to stay

and if by night my sorrow pales
morning dew my heart avails
with no sound I hear You speak
Your glory aches
my bones fall weak

not alone I suffer still
when towards Your might I climb this hill
no earthly shade to quench this fire
unending love my Lord transpires

when my body steps aside
mind and soul do open wide
my will to Yours be true and tried
beyond my slumber now abide

the dove will fly above the wire
and seal my soul with sound desire
I pray to breathe Your healing fire
Oh Holy Spirit descend, inspire

End Notes

Below are the passages from Sacred Scripture (NRSV Bible) and other sources that influenced some of the prayers and poems:

12 Hours of Daylight

John 11: 9-10
9 Jesus answered, "Are there not twelve hours of daylight? Those who walk during the day do not stumble, because they see the light of this world. 10 But those who walk at night stumble, because the light is not in them."

Prophet Named

(Note: Narrator of poem is the collective Old Testament prophet)

Book of Daniel 3, 5 & 6

Daniel 14:27
Then Daniel took some pitch, fat, and hair; these he boiled together and made into cakes. He put them into the mouth of the dragon, and when the dragon ate them, he burst. "This," he said, "is what you revered."

Ezekiel 37:3 -7
3 He said to me, "Mortal, can these bones live?" I answered, "O Lord God, you know." 4 Then he said to me, "Prophesy to these bones, and say to them: O dry bones, hear the word of the Lord. 5 Thus says the Lord God to these bones: I will cause

breath[a] to enter you, and you shall live. 6 I will lay sinews on you, and will cause flesh to come upon you, and cover you with skin, and put breath[b] in you, and you shall live; and you shall know that I am the Lord."

7 So I prophesied as I had been commanded; and as I prophesied, suddenly there was a noise, a rattling, and the bones came together, bone to its bone.

Rend to Render

Ephesians 1:18
...so that, with the eyes of your heart enlightened, you may know what is the hope to which he has called you, what are the riches of his glorious inheritance among the saints.

Curse to Bless

Genesis 12:3
I will bless those who bless you, and the one who curses you I will curse; and in you all the families of the earth shall be blessed.

The Book of Joel 2 & 3

Micah 4:3
He shall judge between many peoples, and shall arbitrate between strong nations far away;
they shall beat their swords into plowshares, and their spears into pruning hooks; nation shall not lift up sword against nation, neither shall they learn war any more...

Towards the Fire

Matthew 5:9
Blessed are the peacemakers, for they will be
called the children of God.

Wandering

Philippians 4:13
I can do all things through him who strengthens
me.

Sighs Too Deep

Romans 8:26 - 27
Likewise the Spirit helps us in our weakness; for
we do not know how to pray as we ought, but that
very Spirit intercedes with sighs too deep for
words. 27 And God, who searches the heart, knows
what is the mind of the Spirit, because the Spirit
intercedes for the saints according to the will of
God.

Onto All That is Ordinary

Proverbs 14:33
Wisdom is at home in the mind of one who has
understanding, but it is not known in the heart of
fools.

Lead Me to Discern

What is Ignatian Spirituality? by David L.
Flemming, SJ (Chapter 1)

Pointing Past Forward

Mark 14:51-52
51 A certain young man was following him, wearing nothing but a linen cloth. They caught hold of him, 52 but he left the linen cloth and ran off naked.

John 20: 3-7
3 Then Peter and the other disciple set out and went toward the tomb. 4 The two were running together, but the other disciple outran Peter and reached the tomb first. 5 He bent down to look in and saw the linen wrappings lying there, but he did not go in. 6 Then Simon Peter came, following him, and went into the tomb. He saw the linen wrappings lying there, 7 and the cloth that had been on Jesus' head, not lying with the linen wrappings but rolled up in a place by itself.

Like the Father

BULL OF INDICTION OF THE
EXTRAORDINARY JUBILEE OF MERCY
8 December 2015- 20 November 2016
"Merciful Like the Father" Pope Francis

To Contact Author: cradlepress@yahoo.com

Pressing Olives may be purchased online at:
Amazon.com
BarnesandNoble.com

(or ordered at your local bookstore)

www.ingramcontent.com/pod-product-compliance
Lightning Source LLC
Chambersburg PA
CBHW020952030426
42339CB00004B/57